Edward Carpenter

1

432

Edwd Carpenter

EDWARD CARPENTER:
POET AND PROPHET

BY

ERNEST Howard CROSBY

Author of "Plain Talk in Psalm and Parable"

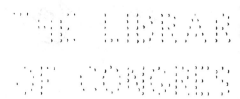

1901

THE CONSERVATOR

PHILADELPHIA

Next follows the explanation of the Infinite as the Self; Self is below, above, behind, before, right and left—Self is all this.

He who sees, perceives, and understands this, loves the Self, delights in the Self, revels in the Self, rejoices in the Self—he becomes an autocrat; he is lord and master in all the worlds. . . .

But those who think differently from this, live in perishable worlds, and have other beings for their rulers.—*Khandogya-Upanishad, VII, 25.*

He who beholds all beings in the Self, and the Self in all beings, he never turns away from it.

When to a man who understands, the Self has become all things, what sorrow, what trouble can there be to him who once beheld that unity?—*Vagasaneyi-Samhita-Upanishad, 6-7.*

EDWARD CARPENTER: POET AND PROPHET

Prophets usually have the defects of their good qualities. They are often narrow, intolerant and over strenuous, and they rarely possess a saving sense of humor. Edward Carpenter is, however, a conspicuous exception ; he is without question a prophet, but in his writings at any rate he has escaped these failings of his order. There is a sweet reasonableness in his wildest assertions, and a twinkle of merriment in his eye when his thought is at its deepest, that are intensely refreshing to one who loves prophets and yet wearies at times of their stress and strain. One hallmark of the prophet he emphatically has : he is without honor in his own country ; for the high measure of fame which he enjoys among a few choice souls, who would generally be classed as cranks, could hardly be called honor in the acceptation of the bookmongers of the day. True, one of his volumes is in the fifth edition, but it is quite safe to assert that neither Lord Salisbury nor Mr. Chamberlain nor the Archbishop of Canterbury is familiar with its contents ; and it is amusing to read in the list of essays in another book the names of the obscure and defunct journals in which they first appeared, during a period in which the standard reviews were printing the usual mass of rubbish, little conscious that they were turning their backs upon noteworthy contributions to the permanent literature of England.   Carpenter is a lecturer, too, as well as an author and poet, but dukes do not take the chair when he appears on the platform, nor does "society" throng him.   He is rather to be found talking in dimly lighted rooms to a score or two of workingmen.

Yet the world had every reason to give Carpenter a good reception   He was a Brahmin of the Brahmins, born in easy circumstances at Brighton, in 1844, educated at Cambridge, a fellow of his college, and for some time curate under Frederick Denison Maurice.   But he soon threw up his fellowship and relinquished orders, devoting himself to the duties of a university extension lecturer on science and music.   Leaves of Grass made a profound impression upon him, and in 1877, and again in 1884, he made pilgrimages to the home of Walt Whitman, at Camden, New Jersey, finding the poet still greater than his works.   Overcome with disgust for the civilization which hedged him in from the mass of his fellowmen, and falling in love with the classes that do the hard work of the world, Carpenter went in 1881 to share a laborer's cottage near Sheffield, and to work with him in the fields.   There he lives still, passing a part of the year with a mechanic in the neighboring city, where he has built up a considerable business in the manufacture of sandals, of which I shall have more to say hereafter. Meanwhile he writes poetry and prose and lectures on matters social and economic. In short, Carpenter loves his nighbor in deed as well as in word, and has of necessity ceased to be respectable. His so-called college "fellowship" was reputable, and from that post his writings might have reached polite society (as Ruskin's did), but the fellow of Yorkshire farm and factory hands ! how could the world be expected to listen to such a man ?

Carpenter's first and greatest work, Towards Democracy, appeared in 1883, and a third edition of it, containing many additions, came out in 1892. It is a collection of poems in the rhymeless, rhythmless form of Whitman, and in it he has given the strongest and most emotional expression to his inner vision. In 1887 he printed several papers in book form under the title, England's Ideal, and two years later followed Civilization, Its Cause and Cure, another volume of essays. His Love's Coming of Age, with a supplementary pamphlet, presents his views on the relation of the sexes, while Angels' Wings gives his conception of art and music. These books, taken together, with a book of travels in India, and various articles in magazines, form the present corpus of his work—a unique achievement, unconventional, original, thoughtful, brilliant, and not to be

ignored.   They possess the vital spark and may be content to come into notice slowly, like the sprout from the
tiny pineseed in a field of overgrown weeds.

Carpenter is forever to be associated with Whitman.
The two men differ from each other and yet it is not
easy to point out the difference.   They have practically
the same '' welt-anschauüng'' or world-conception, as
the Germans so expressively say.   We for the most part
lack comprehensive conceptions of the world as well as
a term for them, but Whitman and Carpenter are both
farsighted beyond their fellows and they preserve a sim-
ilar and consistent point of view.   They see life as a`
great and transcendent unity, welling up in innumerable
forms but always in effect the same, entitled to the same
reverence and love, and their hearts go forth to this life.
Whitman found himself gazing at the world from this
new outlook with the unreasoning astonishment of a
child, and he blurted what he saw with a force and
originality which can never be surpassed.   Carpenter
saw the same sight but he knew what he saw ; he has
the great advantage—and the great disadvantage—of self
consciousness.   He sees what Whitman sees, but he
also sees something of the reason of it.   He naturally
classifies and deduces and forms the outlines of a system,
while Whitman, when he undertakes in prose to give the
upshot of his poetry, fails signally to appreciate its im-
port.   Leaves of Grass is the impassioned cry of a bright

child as he first sees the beauties of his father's new house and garden. Carpenter's books embody the poetry and philosophy of a mature man who knows a little about horticulture and masonry and can comprehend the adaptation of houses and gardens to their uses. The difference is perhaps one rather of education than of genius, but we may be thankful for it, for the world scarcely requires another Whitman yet, while there was need for a calmer and more comprehensive view of the landmarks of the new world. Of course, in surmising that Carpenter sees just what Whitman saw, I do not mean at all to doubt the former's originality. I have yet, however, to find a line in Leaves of Grass to which I should not expect the author of Towards Democracy to give his fullest assent. The sympathy of the younger for the older poet is complete, and in two articles which he has written describing his visits to Walt's home at Camden, he has, as it seems to me, shown more insight into the character of the old man, and the hard-fought struggles which it summed up, than any other writer whom I can recall.*

To do justice to an author we must attempt to catch something of his spirit, and it is in his poems, contained in Towards Democracy, that Carpenter's spirit and character show themselves most clearly. The name of the book is the worst thing about it. To feel its signifi-

---

* Progressive Review, London, 1897

cance we must go back to the France of the eighteenth century, when democracy was still a dream and when the name had not been debased by association with discouraging experiments and narrow parties. We must conclude from Carpenter's use of the term "democracy" that its original polish has not worn off as completely in England as it has in America.* He certainly had not in mind its etymological derivation, as implying the rule of the people in any sense by majority votes, representative institutions or the initiative and referendum. I can only ascribe his infelicitous choice of a title to the common weakness shown by distinguished writers in naming their literary offspring.†

The long series of poems in Towards Democracy is with few exceptions written in the Whitmanesque meter, or lack of meter. I do not regard this fact as a sign of imitation but rather of the natural adaptation of this style to the new and fresh conception of the universe which is common to both poets. The trim balance of a Christmas tree with its colored candles and gilt balls and stars

---

* We hold the words of our language in trust for posterity What breaches of trust lie at our door ! We might trace the story of a nation's decadence in its successive dictionaries The words "tyrant" and "despot" were once honorable

† The names of most of Shakespeare's comedies might be drawn from a hat and applied indiscriminately without in any way injuring their effectiveness The titles of Kipling's best stories seem to bear slight relationship to their contents His book, Mine Own People, begins with the story of an ape ! I fear this was an unconscious adoption of the lower animals as brothers

is beautiful in its way, but the very want of symmetry
helps to make the oak and the pine kings of the forest.
And it is out of doors and into the forest that the new
love of nature drives men—away from the orderly courts
of princes into the tumult of the market place.   Even
blank verse with all its grandeur is too suggestive of
landscape gardening and the studied roughness of "rock
gardens."   When Carpenter tries it he does not succeed, and he tells us that he feels obliged to write his
poetry in the open air, for indoors it will insist on rhym-
ing and rhythming.   He wishes it to be instinct with
the life of nature, to represent the "serene, untampered
facts of earth and sky" (Towards Democracy, p. 16.)
As he says in a later poem (After Long Ages, Towards
Democracy, p 247) :

Great ragged clouds wild over the sky careering, pass
changing, shifting through my poems !
Blow, O breezes, mingle, O winds, with these words
—whose purpose is the same as yours !

Clouds and winds will not submit to architectural art,
nor will the deep cry for brotherhood and unity which
Whitman and Carpenter both utter.   It is idle to call
their poetry formless ; it creates its own form and refuses
to crawl into the chrysalis of earlier verse.   On the first
page of his poems Carpenter strikes, as in an overture,
the various motifs of his work.   "Deep as the universe is my life," he cries, and then

Freedom ! the deep breath ! the word heard centuries and centuries beforehand : the soul singing low and passionate to itself · Joy ! joy !

Freedom and joy in the life universal : that is the message of Carpenter ; and who will say that there is a better one for the world of today? The poet has felt the world's need and experienced it, and he has found the remedy springing up at the bottom of his heart, and now he comes to share his discovery with his fellow-men.

The gates are thrown wide open all through the universe.   I go to and fro—through the heights and depths I go and I return :   All is well.   (Towards Democracy, p. 5.)

This universality of life makes the lowest equal to the highest.

If I am not level with the lowest, I am nothing. (Towards Democracy, p. 6.)

To descend, first :
To feel downwards and downwards through this wretched maze of shame for the solid ground—to come close to the Earth itself and those who live in direct contact with it.
To identify, to saturate yourself with these, . . .
This . . . is the first thing.   (Towards Democracy, p. 28.)

Are you laughed at, are you scorned?
My, child, there is One that not only thinks of you,

but who cannot at all get on without you.   (Towards
Democracy, p. 34.)

In Carpenter's case this sympathy for the lowly does
not come as a deduction from the oneness of life ;
rather was it through this sympathy that he found the
great all-inclusive life ; it was the clue to the secret.   In
the midst of the artificial existence of his class he had
been oppressed by the shams and conventions which
hemmed him in.   In the drawing room, in the street, at
the railway station, he could not escape them.

Was this then the sum of life ?
A grinning, gibbering organization of negations—a
polite trap, and circle of endlessly complaisant faces
bowing you back from reality ! . . .
Well, as it happened just then—and as we stopped at
a small way station—my eyes from their swoon-sleep
opening, encountered the grimy and oil-besmeared figure
of a stoker.
Close at my elbow on the footplate of his engine he
was standing, devouring bread and cheese
And the fire-light fell on him brightly as for a moment
his eyes rested on mine.
That was all, but it was enough.
The youthful face, yet so experienced and calm, was
enough ;
The quiet look, the straight untroubled unseeking
eyes, resting upon me—giving me without any ado the
thing I needed . . .

For in a moment I felt the sting and torrent of Reality.

The swift nights out in the rain I felt, and the great black sky overhead, and the flashing of red and green lights in the forward distance.

The anxious straining for a glimpse sideways into the darkness—cap tied tightly on—the dash of cold and wet above, the heat below—

All this I felt, as if it had been myself. . . .

O eyes, O face, how in that moment without any ado you gave me all !

How in a moment the whole vampire brood of flat paralytic faces fled away, and you gave me back the great breasts of Nature, when I was rejected of others and like to die of starvation. (Towards Democracy, pp. 140–3)

It was when confronted with men such as the stoker that Carpenter's soul found its bearings : in "society" so called he felt himself hopelessly adrift. In his Sunday Morning After Church he gives a description of the aimless well dressed mob on the esplanade at a watering place, and as he sits watching them he closes his eyes for an instant, and visions of the naked and outcast rise before him :

The mother snatches some half-pence from her boy matchseller and makes for the nearest gin-shop ; squalid streets and courts are in the background and filthy workshops ; . . .

I open my eyes again. The gay crowd still glides past, exchanging greetings, the flounces and lace are still on the chair beside me. I catch the fluffy smell.

I rise and pass down towards the sea. It lies there, unnoticed as before, slate-green and solemn, stretching miles and miles away ; but the wind has risen and is rising, and in the distance here and there it is fretful with sharp white teeth. (Towards Democracy, 115–18.)

A world which ignored the misery upon which its prosperity was founded, and which denied the essential unity of the poor and criminal with itself, was a hollow imposture and Carpenter would have none of it.

The reader may have remarked in these extracts that Carpenter has Whitman's power of calling up a scene vividly in a few words. Here are other examples :

I hear the sound of the whetting of scythes.

The beautiful grass stands tall in the meadows, mixed with sorrel and buttercups ; the steamships move on across the sea, leaving trails of distant smoke. I see the tall white cliffs of Albion. (Towards Democracy, p. 52.)

The drunken father reeling home in the rain across country—he has more than a mile to go—singing, cursing, tumbling hands and knees in the mire—the son following unbeknown at a little distance (he has been watching a long time for his father outside the beershop); the late moon rising on the strange scene, the hiccuped oaths of the old man through the silence of the night. (Towards Democracy, p. 71.)

The baffling infant face, with closed eyes and flexible upper lip, and storms and sunshine sweeping across its tiny orb, and filmy clouds of expression. (Towards Democracy, p. 302.)

The aged grandmother sits in the ruddy glow of the chimney-corner—her little grandson leans against her knee—

The other children (for some have come in from the neighboring cottage, and Christmas is now approaching) sing hymn after hymn in tireless trebles, and the old grand-dad tones the bass in now and then with still melodious voice :

While silent, with tired and suffering face (thinking of the week's work and of her runaway drunken husband) the mother strips her youngest naked in the firelight. (Towards Democracy, p. 302.)

This same power of description is shown conspicuously in Carpenter's picture of the steerage of a transatlantic liner and its occupants (Towards Democracy, p. 203 et sequ) and in his lifelike survey of the different parts of England, modeled on Whitman's bird'seye view of the American States. (Towards Democracy, pp. 52–58.)

The key to Carpenter's philosophy lies in the history of his experience. Rebelling as we have seen against the false restraints of the unreal society in which he lived, he found his outlet into the universal life of those who were humblest and nearest to nature. In the consciousness of the life universal thus acquired he assumes another standpoint and sees all things new. His sympathy, his love, react upon him in the form of a revelation, and it is a transfigured love, supreme over death and fate, which he is now inspired to sing :

Because thou rulest, O glorious, and before thee all else fails,
And at thy dread new command—at thy word Democracy—the children of the earth and the sea and the sky find their voices, and the despised things come forth and rejoice ;
Because in thy arms, O strong one, I laugh death to scorn—nay I go forth to meet him with gladness,   . .
Because out of disallowed and unaccepted things—and always out of these—full-armed and terrific,
Like a smiting and consuming flame, O Love, O Democracy,
Even out of the faces and bodies of the huge and tameless multitudes of the Earth—
A great ocean of fire with myriad tongues licking the vault of heaven,
Thou arisest—
Therefore, O Love, O Flame, wherein I burning die and am consumed—carried aloft to the stars a disembodied voice—
O dread Creator and Destroyer,
Do I praise Thee. (Towards Democracy, pp. 170–1.)

Passing by, passing by all exteriors,
Swimming, floating on the Ocean that has innumerable bays—

I too at length nestle down in thy breast, O humanity;
Tired, I abandon myself to thee, to be washed from the dust of life in thy waves.   (Towards Democracy, p. 332.)

In one of his most beautiful poems he develops this idea :

All night by the shore, . . .
I am a bit of the shore : the waves feed upon me, they come pasturing over me ; . . .
I am a little arm of the sea ; the same tumbling, swooning dream goes on—I feel the waves all around me, I spread myself through them. . . .
I am detached, I disentangle myself from the shore : I have become free—I float out and mingle with the rest. . . .
Suddenly I am the great living Ocean itself—the awful Spirit of Immensity creeps over my face.
I am in love with it.   All night and ages and ages long and for ever I pour my soul out to it in love.
I spread myself out broader and broader forever, that I may touch it and be with it everywhere.
I know but I do not care any longer which my own particular body is—all conditions and fortunes are mine.
By the ever beautiful coast-line of human life, by all shores, in all climates and countries, by every secluded nook and inlet,
Under the eye of my beloved Spirit I glide :
O joy ! forever, ever joy !   (Towards Democracy, p. 158.)

And this "expanded identity" (Towards Democracy, p. 158) which is Carpenter's root thought is felt now and does not wait for death.

O death, I shall conquer thee yet. . . .

Long, long years ago did I not abandon this frail tenement, all but in name ?—was not my last furniture packed up and ready to be transported ?

The virgin grass received me, and the beech trees so tenderly green in Spring, and the bodies of my lovers that I loved ; . . .

I passed freely and floated on the ocean of which I had only been part of the shore. (Towards Democracy, pp. 329–330.)

It is no wonder that a man who has passed through such feelings should be blest with universal sympathies, especially towards the humble and simple. Carpenter is devoted to the children of the poor ; again and again in his poetry we meet the "little ragged boy" (Towards Democracy, p. 145), "the pale smudged face, . . . the curls fringing his dirty cap." (Towards Democracy, p. 150) For him the inanimate world, too, is alive and to be loved as a living thing The very air, "the dainty sweet air," is to him "the outbreath of innumerable creatures." There is, however, apparently, one exception to his rule of universal love. Carpenter has little affection for the Pharisee—the respectable, pious, well-to-do individual who thinks that the lower classes are made to serve as his pedestal.

I come forth from the darkness to smite Thee—
Who art thou, insolent of all the earth,
With thy faint sneer for him who wins thee bread
And him who clothes thee, and for him who toils
Daylong and nightlong dark in the earth for thee?
Coward without a name ! (Towards Democracy, p.
130.)

The evil in the Pharisee is almost the only evil which
he recognizes. Our passions are good in themselves,
but we must not let them rule us.

For (over and over again) there is nothing that is evil
except because a man has not mastery over it ; and there
is no good thing that is not evil if it have mastery over
a man. . . .
Things cannot be divided into good and evil, but all
are good so soon as they are brought into subjection.
(Towards Democracy, p 362.)

When thy body—as needs must happen at times—is
carried away on the wind of passion, say not thou "I
desire this or that :"
For the "I" neither desires nor fears anything, but
is free and in everlasting glory, dwelling in heaven and
pouring out joy like the sun on all sides.
Let not that precious thing by any confusion be drawn
down and entangled in the world of opposites, and of
death and suffering. (Towards Democracy, p. 346.)

The body is to be honored as well as the soul ; it is
even the "latest and best gift long concealed from men."

Let the strong desires come and go ; refuse them not, disown them not ; but think not that in them lurks finally the thing you want.

Presently they will fade away and into the intolerable light will dissolve like gossamers before the sun. (Towards Democracy, p. 172.)

The old moral rules which required a man to suppress his instincts resulted in the production of "slaves of chastity, slaves of unchastity." Carpenter's aim is beyond all that :

Passing the boundaries of evil, being delivered, being filled with joy, . . .

Content, overjoyed, knowing that I have yet far to go ; but that all is open and free and that Thou wilt provide—

Gladly, O gladly, I surrender myself to Thee.   Towards Democracy, 253.)

The advantage which Carpenter enjoys in the rhythmic form which he has chosen for his work lies chiefly in its wide range.   He can, when the subject matter demands it, write in the baldest prose, and choose, if he please, the language of the streets, but again he can give us the purest music.   Towards Democracy has the merits of both prose and poetry and the two run into each other imperceptibly and without a break.   The new poetry of democracy needs an instrument of wider register and Whitman and Carpenter have found it.   The form is

poetical whenever the sentiment demands it.   Who fails
to hear music in these lines for instance ?

High in my chamber I hear the deep bells chime—
Midnight.
The great city sleeps with arms outstretched, supine
under the stars—deep-breathing, hushed—
Into the kennels of sleep are gone the loud-baying
cares of day, and hunted man rests for a moment. . . .
To the waking fever of remorse ;
To the long cadaverous vigil of physical pain ;
And to the long vigil of the heart-broken wife praying
vainly for respite from thought ;
The hour swings onward.
High in heaven over the supine city—over the wilder-
ness of roofs beneath the stars—
The hour swings surely onward.   (Towards Democ-
racy, pp. 119–120.)

Carpenter is indeed more often a poet in the conven-
tional acceptance of the term—is more nearly related to
Shelley and Poe, in form at least—than is Walt Whitman.

Carpenter finds a microcosm in himself and constructs
a history of the world from his own experience.   Scien-
tists have declared that the record of life on this planet
for hundreds of thousands of years may be read in the
development of a single fetus ; Carpenter as clearly and
as scientifically deciphers it in the biography of his consciousness.   Just as he was bound hand and foot by the

customs and prejudices of his class, just as he burst forth into comparative freedom, so the history of all life is a history of imprisonment by the ossified forms of the past and of the breaking forth of the new life to the light and air, and of the casting aside of the outworn husk.

Lo! the Conscience, the tender green shoot in each one, growing, arising, Ygdrasil casting its leaves, elements and nations over the universe!
Lo! the moral laws so long swathing the soul, loosing, parting at last for the liberation of that which they prepared. (Towards Democracy, p. 105.)
I choke! . . .
(The natural sheath protecting the young bud—fitting close, stranglingly close, till the young thing gains a little more power, and then falling dry, useless, to the ground.)
Strangled, O God? Nay—the circle of gibbering faces draws closer, the droning noises become louder, the weight gets heavier, unbearable—One instant struggle! and lo!
It is over!—daylight! the sweet rain is falling and I hear the songs of birds. (Towards Democracy, p. 27.)

And he sees the same change effected in others :

I saw a vision of Earth's multitudes going up and down over the Earth—and I saw the great Earth itself wheeling and careering onward through space.
And behold! here and there to one among the multitude a change came ;

And to whomsoever it came continued onward as before—yet as from the larva springs the perfect image,
So (as it appeared to me) from the mortal form a new
being—long, long, long in preparation—glided silently
up unobserved into the breathless pure height of the sky.
(Towards Democracy, pp. 332–3.)

In his fine poem After Long Ages, perhaps his most
significant work (Towards Democracy, pp. 218–258), he
develops this idea in its wider bearings :

This is the order of man and of history ;
Descending he runs to and fro over the world, and
dwells (for a time) among things that have no sense ;
Forgetful of his true self he becomes a selfseeker
among the shadows.
But out of these spring only war and conflict and
tangling of roots and branches ;
And things which have no sense succeed things which
have no sense—for nothing can have any sense but by
reason of that of which it is the shadow—and one phan-
tasmal order follows another—and one pleasure or in-
dulgence another—and one duty or denial another—
Till, bewildered and disgusted, finding no rest, no
peace, but everywhere only disappointment,
He returns (and History returns) seeking for that
which is.
Toilsome and long is the journey ; shell after shell,
envelope after envelope, he discards,
Over the mountains, over the frowning barriers, un-
daunted, unwrapping all that detains him.

Enduring poverty, brother of the outcast and of animals, enduring ridicule and scorn,

Through vast morasses, by starlight and dawn, through dangers and labors and nakedness, through chastity and giving away all that he has, through long night watches on the mountains and washings in the sunlit streams and sweet food untainted by blood, through praises and thanks and joy ascending before him—

All, all conventions left aside, all limitations passed, all shackles dropped—the husks and sheaths of ages falling off—

At length the Wanderer returns to heaven. (Towards Democracy, pp. 234-5.)

The poem After Long Ages is indeed the poetical expression of Carpenter's philosophy of history, which he has set forth more systematically in an essay on Civilization. Its Cause and Cure, the initial paper in his book of that name. His prose naturally appeals to a much larger audience than his poetry. Those who are unacquainted with his writings and have no special predilection for ''prose-poems'' should first read this volume of essays, which for originality and brilliancy it would be hard to match in recent literature. We are accustomed to look upon our modern civilization, with its machinery, its overgrown cities, its noise and bustle, as a kind of finality, and upon the life of the future as an indefinite advance in the same direction, but Car-

penter undertakes to prove from history that the present
is only a temporary stage of development, like all
former civilizations, involving much evil as well as good
—in fact, a "kind of disease which the various races of
men have to pass through, as children pass through
measles or whooping cough." (Civilization : Its Cause
and Cure, p. 1.) That disease, mental as well as physical, is particularly prevalent among civilized peoples is
certainly true. The earlier stages of evolution, savagery
and barbarism, were at least comparatively healthy.
The primary cause of the change from barbarism to
civilization seems to be the gradual recognition of private
property as distinguished from communal ownership.
The old power of the clan gives way to a society of
classes founded upon differences of wealth. Slavery,
serfdom and the wagesystem follow, rent and interest
spring up, and with these and to protect them come the
state and the policeman. A glance at the great civilizations
of the world shows that they generally flourish for about
one thousand years. Among the unhealthy symptoms
which mark this period with us is the "sense of sin,"
which, however useful it may be in securing progress, is
in itself surely a morbid indication. The legends of a
Golden Age go to prove that the race remembers a time
when its mind was more at peace with itself. From this
point Carpenter investigates the true meaning of
"health," a term which really denotes a positive

"wholeness" and unity, rather than the mere negative absence of disease which is the ideal of the medical profession. His idea of health is that of a man at one with himself, the soul reigning at the center over the body and holding all passions and desires in proper subjection. Disease is an insubordinate center establishing itself in opposition to the true center of life. When the rebellious center gains the upper hand we have death, but such a death is far from being the euthanasia which should usher man into the unseen future.

Death is simply the loosening and termination of the action of this power over certain regions of the organism, a process by which, when these superficial parts become hardened and osseous, as in old age, or irreparably damaged, as in cases of accident, the inward being sloughs them off and passes into other spheres. In the case of man there may be noble and there may be ignoble death, as there may be noble and ignoble life. The inward self, unable to maintain authority over the forces committed to its charge, declining from its high prerogative, swarmed over by parasites, and fallen partially into the clutch of obscene foes, may at last with shame and torment be driven forth from the temple in which it ought to have been supreme. Or, having fulfilled a holy and wholesome time, having radiated divine life and love through all the channels of body and mind, and as a perfect workman uses his tools, so having with perfect mastery and nonchalence used all the materials committed to it, it may quietly and peacefully lay these down, and unchanged (absolutely unchanged to all but material eyes) pass on to other spheres appointed. (Ib. 17.)

Why should man at the very moment of his highest development in civilization lose the healthy unity which prevails in lower forms of life? The cause, Carpenter tells us, is self-knowledge. "Man has to become conscious of his destiny—to lay hold of and realize his freedom and blessedness—to transfer his consciousness from the outer and mortal part of him to the inner and undying." (Ib. 22.) The human soul "has in fact to face the frightful struggle of self-consciousness, or the disentanglement of the true self from the fleeting and perishable self." (Ib. 24) This self-knowledge "is a temporary perversion, indicating the disunion of the present-day man—the disunion of the outer self from the inner—the horrible dual self-consciousness—which is the means of a more perfect and conscious union than could ever have been realized without it." (Ib. 25.) The rôle of private property in bringing about this state of affairs is clear enough—it tends to separate him "from nature, from his true self, from his fellows." (Ib. 27) It surrounds him with an artificial environment, it induces him to live in his possessions rather than in himself, and it gives him a selfish position among his neighbors. It stimulates the consciousness of a false self, for "the true self of man consists in his organic relation with the whole body of his fellows. . . The mass-Man must rule in each unit-man, else the unit-man will drop off and die.'' (Ib. 28.) Before ''the delusion that man can exist for himself alone '' (Ib. 30), the tribal and community life disappears and modern governments take their place. Through monarchy, oligarchy and finally anarchic democracy, society loses its sense of unity, the central inspiration departs from social life, and the body politic falls a prey to parasites which devour it.

But this is no true Democracy. Here in this '' each for himself'' is no rule of the Demos in every man, nor anything resembling it. . . . The true Democracy has yet to come. Here in this present stage is only the final denial of all outward and class government, in preparation for the restoration of the inner and true authority. Here in this stage the task of civilization comes to an end ; the purport and object of all these centuries is fulfilled ; the bitter experience that mankind has to pass through is completed ; and out of this Death, and all the torture and unrest which accompanies it, comes at last the Resurrection. Man has sounded the depths of alienation from his own divine spirit, he has drunk the dregs of the cup of suffering, he has literally descended into Hell ; henceforth he turns, both in the individual and in society, and mounts deliberately and consciously back again towards the unity which he has lost. And the false Democracy parts aside for the disclosure of the true Democracy which has been formed beneath it— which is not an external government at all, but an inward rule—the rule of the mass-Man in each unit-man.* For no outward government can be anything but a make-shift—a temporary hard chrysalis-sheath to hold the grub together while the new life is forming inside.   (Ib. 33–4.)

And so in his prose as in his poetry Carpenter returns to the powerful simile, which is not all a simile, of the husk, the sheath, the chrysalis—the narrow ossified representative of ancient life, protecting and yet tending to suffocate the new life formed within, and at last thrown off by it, the same process to be ever repeated as long as the universe lives and grows.   To this throwing off of the husk he applies a term of Whitman's, "exfoliation," and he shows that "the process of evolution or exfoliation itself is nothing but a continual unclothing of Nature, by which the perfect human form which is at the root of it comes nearer and nearer to its manifestation."   (Ib. 36).   He gives at the end of his book a separate essay on Exfoliation, so strongly has the idea impressed itself upon his imagination.   In it he studies evolution in himself, as the entity best known to him, and finds that the most important factor in variation must be sought in an inner law of growth and not in environment.

Every change begins in the mental region—is felt first

---

* Dhammapada, chap XII, v 160   " Self is the lord of self, who else could be the lord ?"—Sacred Books of the East.

in a desire gradually taking form in thought, passes down into the bodily region, expresses itself in action (more or less dependent on conditions), and finally solidifies itself in organization and structure. The process is not accretive but exfoliatory—a continual movement from within outwards. (Ib. 138.)

So in society today

a dim feeling of discontent pervades all ranks and classes. A new sense of justice, of fraternity, has descended among us, which is not satisfied with mere chatter of demand and supply. For a long time this new sentiment or desire remains vague and unformed, but at last it resolves itself into shape ; it takes intellectual form, books are written, plans formed ; then after a time definite new organizations, for the distinct purpose of expressing these ideas, begin to exist in the body of the old society ; and before so very long the whole outer structure of society will have been reorganized by them. (Ib. 139.)

And all this takes place in the same way as in physical organisms. Desire is then the motive force in creation. And "what then is desire—what is its culmination and completion in man? Practically it is love. Love is the sum and solution of all desires in man." (Ib. 141.)

This love, according to Carpenter, is "a worship of and desire for the human form. In our bodies it is a desire for the bodily human form ; in our interior selves it is a perception and worship of an ideal human form, it is the revelation of a Splendor dwelling in others, which—clouded and dimmed as it inevitably may come to be—remains after all one of the most real, perhaps the most real, of the facts of existence.'' (Ib. 141.) The ideal which is sought thus becomes the cause of the forms which precede it. The real motive power in any series of phenomena is the last in point of time to unfold and reveal itself, and the monkey is not the cause of the man but the man of the monkey. Carpenter gives as an example the case of a volcanic eruption in which the cause of all the commotion, the subterranean fire, appears last of all. A new idea in like manner may upheave the surface of society for a long time before it can take visible shape in a new order of things. '' The work of each age is not to build *on* the past, but to rise *out* of the past and throw it off.'' (Ib. 144.) Our author concludes that the real cause of any given thing is not to be found so much preceding it as under it and on another plane, as, for instance, the bricks are not the cause of the house but rather the idea of the house is the cause of the bricks made for it. One grouping of atoms cannot cause another subsequent one, but both are ''determined by a third something which does not belong to quite the same order of existence as the said atoms.'' (Ib. 142.) To discover the relations of leaves on a tree to each other, we must go to the root, and a science which sees only the surface is necessarily shallow. The key to evolution lies in the "ultimate disclosure of the ideal man," and in him alone, at the end of the unfolding and exfoliations, will be revealed the cause and explanation of all that went before.

The true development of man consists, then, in a gradual unfolding, as in the case of a flower ; he must cast off in due time the old customs and institutions which have ceased to be useful and now only serve to hamper his progress. In an almost literal sense Carpenter would have him unclothe himself, or at any rate simplify his clothing—for he has little patience with the garments now dictated by fashion, the top-hat, starched shirt and collar, and foot-disfiguring boot. He pictures man as he retires from the simplicity of nature, clothing himself in apparel "more and more fearfully and wonderfully fashioned, till he ceases to be recognizable as the man that was once the crown of the animals, and presents a more ludicrous appearing spectacle than the monkey that sits on his own barrel-organ." (Ib. 26.)

Carpenter would persuade man to return to a more natural life, rather out of doors than shut up in the "boxes with breathing holes which he calls houses," eating plainer food, vegetable rather than animal, and preserving the natural power of his nerves and muscles by the rational exercise of useful physical labor. Nor does he fear any relapse to barbarism from the adoption of such an ideal. There would be more humanity and sociability, more true art and beauty, than ever. All the appliances of civilization must be "reduced to abject subjection to the real man ;" they must no longer be the object of a mere fetish worship. Men will at last *feel* their unity with each other, with the animals and with the mountains and streams. He who is conscious of being an integral part of the living whole will cease to ask the whither and whence.

For what causes these questions to be asked is simply the wretched feeling of isolation, actual or prospective, which man necessarily has when he contemplates himself as a separate atom in this immense universe—the gulf which lies below seemingly ready to swallow him, and the anxiety to find some mode of escape. But when he feels once more that he, that *he* himself, is absolutely, indivisibly and indestructibly a part of this great whole—why then there is no gulf into which he can possibly fall. (Ib. 46.)

He will become conscious of the "cosmic self." Carpenter sees in the society in which he lives two movements which tend to lead towards the new order, at the same time acting as correctives upon each other, namely, that towards individual freedom and savagery and that towards a complex human communism. In them he sees the hope of the world.

Carpenter criticises most stingingly the scientific temper of the day. He can speak from the book, as he is a man of scientific attainments and representative of the best which the scientific education of Great Britain can afford. In his essays on Modern Science and the Science of the Future he follows in Stallo's* footsteps in challenging the accuracy of the fundamental formulæ of science. He shows that the theory of the law of gravitation is faulty, that we have no idea of the actual course of any planet in space, that such conceptions as that of an atom or of luminiferous ether are nonsense, and that the undulatory theory of light and the so-called laws of the conservation of energy and the survival of the fittest are equally meaningless and absurd. In short, nothing is less certain than the laws of science, and they only seem to work at all in those regions with which we are least familiar. Thus, astronomy is the most exact science because we know the least about it, while psychology can hardly be termed a science at all, because we are face to face with it, see its intricacy and are totally unable to disentangle its laws. The radical mistake which men of science have made consists in their disregard of the human element, of the palpitating life in us which underlies the whole. Science has confined its studies to intellectual phenomena. "She has failed

---

* Concepts and Theories of Modern Physics By J B Stallo. New York D Apoleton & Co , 1882

because she has attempted an impossible task ; for the discovery of a permanently valid and purely intellectual representation of the universe is simply impossible. Such a thing does not exist.'' (Civilization : Its Cause and Cure, p. 52.) The scientist tries to get away from man—to get away, in other words, from that which he knows best in his own consciousness and experience. But the truth is that ''the very facts of Nature, as we call them, are at least half feeling.'' (Ib. 82.) All scientific reasoning begins with axioms which are nothing but feelings, and thought is invariably ''the expression, the outgrowth, the covering of underlying feeling.'' (Ib. 86.) True science, when at last it makes its appearance, will not be an irreverent dissection of Nature, but rather a sympathetic walking with her, ''the life of the open air, and on the land and the waters, the companionship of the animals and the trees and the stars, the knowledge of their habits at first hand.'' (Ib 92.) '' Science has two alternatives before it—either to be merely intellectual and to seek for its star-point in some quite external (and imaginary) thing, like the Atom, or to be divine and to seek for its absolute in innermost recesses of humanity.'' (Ib. 93-4.) It is in the universal consciousness again that Carpenter would place the source and object of true science.

But the most interesting results of Carpenter's convictions, the natural consequence of his consciousness of

universal unity} are to be found in the realm of sociology
and political economy. If he and the criminal are one,
he cannot cast the first stone at the criminal. He demon-
strates in fact that in various ages and nations the standard of morals has ranged from pole to pole. The Spar-
tans applauded lying and theft. In one country the en-
closure of land is a crime, in another it is the trespasser
upon enclosed land who is the criminal. Polygamy is a
sin here and a virtue there. The prevailing code of
morals is always that of the dominant class, and today
morality hinges upon the sanctity of private property.
It will hinge on something higher in the day of brotherhood and equality. Man will reach a loftier plane of
ethics when "he comes to know and *feel* himself a part
of society through his inner nature." The solution
here as in all else lies in the deepening of man's consciousness. Meanwhile the criminal may be performing
a service to society in keeping alive instincts which are
condemned at the present hour, but which may have
been regarded as praiseworthy in other times and which
may be necessary to humanity. The deepening of consciousness means union and love, and "between lovers
there are no duties and rights." (Ib. 124.) When we
feel our oneness with society, there can no longer be a
clashing between our interests and those of the whole of
which we form a part.

How different from all this are the aspirations and

practices of the men who guide society and how skill-
fully Carpenter punctures the bubbles in which they de-
light in his England's Ideal! He perceives that "the
pervading aim and effort of personal life, either consciously or unconsciously entertained, is to maintain our-
selves at the cost of others—to live at the expense of
other folks' labor, without giving an equivalent of our
own labor in return, and," he adds, "if this is not dis-
honesty, I don't know what is!" What is England's
ideal, he asks, and what of all civilized peoples? Is it
not to get as much and give as little as you can? (England's Ideal, pp. 3-5.) Here is the ideal of the popu-
lar fancy—"to live dependent on others, consuming
much and creating next to nothing—to occupy a spa-
cious house, have servants ministering to you, dividends
converging from various parts of the world towards you,
workmen handing you the best part of their labor as
profits, tenants obsequiously bowing as they disgorge
their rent, and a good balance at the bank." And he
shows how for every man who consumes more than he
creates there must be one at least who has to create more
than he consumes. Undue wealth is balanced by undue
poverty. "As far as the palaces of the rich stretch
through Mayfair and Belgravia and South Kensington,
so far (and farther) must the hovels of the poor inevitably stretch in the opposite direction." (Ib. 6.) And
he concludes, as every honest observer must conclude,

that the "whole Gentility business is corrupt through-
out, and will not bear looking into for a moment. It is
incompatible with Christianity (at least as Christ appears
to have taught it) ; it gives a constant lie to the doctrine of human brotherhood. The wretched man who
has got into its toils must surrender that most precious of
all things—the human relation to the mass of mankind."
(Ib. 7.) What is the meaning of an "independence"
by which a man is enabled to cease from labor and to
become absolutely dependent on the labor of others?
Carpenter explains it.

One man accumulates enough money to bring him in a
substantial income—say £500 a year. Then that man
is safe. He has escaped from the labor of feeding himself and his children and may fold his arms and amuse
himself as he likes ; he has got on the dry land beyond
the flood, and this in perpetuity practically. . . Presently
another man accumulates the desired amount. He also
"retires" and is safe. Then a third and fourth. Then
hundreds and thousands, then a considerable portion of
the whole nation—where shall we stop? . . . What is
happening? This is happening—a vast and ever vaster
proportion of the nation is getting by force of existing
rights and machinery to live on the labor of the rest.
Every day, of those who are harnessed to the car of
national life and prosperity, one or another, by dint of
extra forethought, prudence, miserliness, cunning, or
whatever it may be, gets an advantage over the rest,
leaves them, jumps *inside* the car, and thenceforth in-

stead of drawing is drawn. The end is only too obvious. It is a *reductio ad absurdum* of national life. It is break-down, smashup — and the car left in the ditch. (Ib. 26–7.)

Edward Carpenter goes on to prove the wrongfulness of interest, resulting as it does in the formation of an idle, useless class in society. A coat costs naturally the value of the material and the labor bestowed on it ; whence then comes the profit of the capitalist ? It must be deducted from the cost of material or labor, and if full price has been paid for the material, it comes from labor. The result is the overwork and underpay of the laborer who should be able, according to the best au-thorities, to support himself with three or four hours' work a day. Our author investigates the matter of divi-dends from this point of view. The shareholder is a new kind of monster among property owners ; he has no duties, no practical supervision—no knowledge often —of his property ; he does nothing but pocket his share of these unearned "profits." The fact is that the wage earner receives but a fraction of what he produces, a truth which Carpenter establishes at length in his essay on the Meaning of Dividends, and he explains how com-mercial crises arise from this.

Since the wage workers, the mass of the people . . . receive in wages only a portion (say a half) . . . of the value which they actually produce and distribute, it is evident that in any given time, say a year, they will only be able to buy back *one half* of the goods they have thus put on the market during that time. Who then buys the other half of the goods? Clearly not the capitalist and landlord classes. They—though they receive the money credits sufficient to enable them to buy the other half—do not really buy to this amount; for being few in number they cannot possibly use this enormous mass of goods; besides we know as a matter of fact that they save up a large part of their money credits and reinvest them abroad. Hence at the end of the year there remains a mass of goods . . . which is not bought by the masses or by the classes—by the masses because they have not the money—by the classes because they do not want the goods. (England's Ideal 43.)

From this accumulation of unsold goods, increasing every year, results the discharge of wage earners, the formation of an army of unemployed, and all the industrial ills which are ascribed to overproduction. If on the other hand each wage worker received the full value of his labor, there would be for all the products of labor a steady demand which would regulate itself. It is that portion of his earnings which goes to profit, including rent and interest, that causes hard times And what is the permanent result of the "appropriation of balances?"—

an enormous class . . . living in idleness and luxury, they and their children and their children's children, till

they become quite incapable of doing anything for themselves, or even of thinking rightly about most things,
tormented with incurable *ennui* and general imbecility
and futility ; all art and literature which were the ap-
pendage of this class being affected by a kind of St.
Vitus' dance, and the whole thing breaking out finally
for want of any other occupation into a cuff and collar
cult, called respectability.   (Ib. 126.)

And he draws a picture of these respectable people,
living in the " desirable mansions " which we see ad-
vertised in the newspapers, shut out from the real life of
the world and everything done for them, calling themselves educated because they know books, but ignorant
of the plainest and most necessary processes of daily
life and unable to exercise their natural human sympathies towards their neighbors except at arm's length.

By the side of the road there stands a little girl cry-
ing : she has lost her way.   It is very cold, and she
looks pinched and starved.   " Come in, my little girl,
and sit by my cottage fire, and you'll soon get warm ;
and I'll see if I can't find you a bit of something to eat
before you go on. . . . Eh, dear ! how stupid I am— I
quite forgot.   I am sorry I can't ask you in, but I am
living in a desirable mansion now—and though we are
very sorry for you, yet you see we could hardly have
you into our house, for your dirty little boots would
make a dreadful mess of our carpets, and we should
have to dust the chairs after you had sat upon them,
and you see Mrs. Vavasour might happen to come in,

and she would think it so very *odd;* and I know cooks can't bear beggars, and O dear ! I'm so sorry for you— and here's a penny for you, and I hope you'll get home safely." (Ib. 79–80.)

Verily it is easier for a camel to pass through the eye of a needle than for a rich man to enter into those human relations with his fellows which constitute the king- com of heaven ! (Ib. 175.)

The way of escape for the individual lies in simplicity of life and in sharing the manual labor of the world. This will fit him better for the larger affairs which he may be called upon to conduct. What we need is a new ideal of daily life, "some better conception of human dig- nity—such as shall scorn to claim anything for its own which has not been duly earned, and such as shall not find itself degraded by the doing of any work however menial, which is useful to society." (Ib. 72.) And how shall this new ideal be preached ? "There is no need to talk—perhaps the less said about these matters the better—but if you have such new ideal within you, it is I believe your clearest duty, as well as your best inter- est, to act it out in your own life." (Ib. 72.)

There seems but one immediate step that the wealthy despoiler can take—which at the same time is a most obvious step—and that is at once or as soon as ever he can, to place his life on the very simplest footing. And this for several reasons. First, because if he must live

by other people's labor—and in some cases doubtless his
"education" will leave him no other alternative—it is
clearly his duty to consume as little of that commodity
as he possibly can. . . . Secondly, because only by living simply—that is, on a level of simplicity at least equal
to that of the mass of the people—is it possible to know
the people, to become friends with them, to gauge their
wants. . . . Thirdly, because by such a natural life the
cares and anxieties of a luxurious household—the innumerable fidgets and worries and obstacles to all true life,
together with the dread about being able to maintain it
all in the future—are once and for all got rid of. A
great load drops off, and, the Rubicon once crossed, the
difficulties attending the change are seen to be nothing
compared with the increased happiness which it brings.
Fourthly, because it is only on the knowledge and habits
gained in a hard self-supporting life that the higher
knowledge and the fine arts are really founded. (Ib. 176.)

This is the individual ideal, and the social ideal involves the multiplication of such individuals, cooperat-
ing in practical socialism. And he strongly recommends
any course which will further the cause of cooperation
in any way. (Ib 51.)

Thus it is that Carpenter would lead the race on beyond a civilization dominated by private property, while
recognizing the part that such property has played
in the evolution of the past. (England's Ideal 157.)
And what has private ownership become? It is not so
much the right to use as to prevent others from using.

"It is the power to turn all the inhabitants off your land and convert it into a deer forest, or to prevent anyone from tilling any part of your soil. The landlords of England might starve the English people out." (Ib. 141.) The absurdity of such a "right" is self-evident, and yet the same negative principle is involved in all private property. It is not the power to use the property yourself, for you may be quite incapable of cultivating your acres or of using your telescope, and yet you may prevent others, who are anxious to render these things useful to society, from doing so. (Ib. 141.) Real ownership involves mastery of the thing owned and ability to make the best possible use of it ; but this fact is ignored by our laws and customs. It is well that this false ideal of wealth, which Ruskin calls "illth," should be finally rejected and that men should establish a living relationship to their material surroundings. Accumulations of mere "things" are a sign of disease, just as is the accumulation of fat in an over-corpulent man. "It is only when a man enters into the region of equality that a solution offers itself. In finding the true Property of Man he finds the secret of all ownership, and in surrendering all rights of private property, and accepting poverty, he really becomes possessed of all social wealth, and, for the first time, infinitely rich." (Ib. 154.) Once again Carpenter comes back to his central truth :

To build up the Supreme Life in a people—the life of Equality—in which each individual passes out of himself along the lives of his fellows, and in return receives their life into himself with such force that he becomes far greater as an individual than ever before—partaker of the supreme power and well nigh irresistible—to build up this life in a people may well be a task worthy of the combined efforts of poets, philosophers and statesmen. The whole of history and all the age-long struggles of the nations point to its realization.   Even now society like a chrysalis writhes in the birth-throes of the winged creature within.   Equality—the vanishing of the centuries-long conflict between the individual and his fellows—the attainment by each man of a point where all this war of interests ceases to exist, and the barriers which divide man from man are thrown down—this is indeed that Freedom for which all of history has been one long struggle and preparation.   (Ib. 164–5.)

Nor will this equality be a state of dreary monotony, but rather the "equality of the members of the body" fulfilling their various functions in perfect inward harmony.

Does this call to equality require too much self-denial on the part of those who are invited to give up their superfluity? Is there too much of asceticism in the suggestion? Carpenter sees the danger, although he has perhaps made his own life a little too bare in its externals, if we are to believe those who have visited him. While he inculcates moderation in eating, he thinks that "this has to be varied by an occasional orgy. . . . The orgy should not be omitted. Among other things it restores the moral tone and prevents—a very important point—all danger of lapse into pharisaism !'' (Ib. 105.) The same sanity which dictates this unusual advice shows itself again when he sings the praises of love, but he adds : ''When society becomes so altruistic that everybody runs to fetch the coal scuttle, we feel sure that something has gone wrong.'' (Civilization: Its Cause and Cure 113).

We have already noted that Carpenter has no fear for the fate of art in the world of his dreams. Our idea of art as a mere ornament is altogether faulty. ''You cannot *make* your rooms beautiful by buying an expensive vase and putting it on the mantelshelf, but if you live an honest life in it, it will *grow* beautiful in proportion as it comes to answer to the wants of such a life.'' (England's Ideal 109–110.) We must refer the reader to his Angels' Wings, the whimsically named volume in which he treats of art and music, for a full discussion of this question. ''The object of the fine arts,'' he says (and he has read Tolstoi's What Is Art? to good purpose), ''is to convey an emotion.'' (Angels' Wings 42.) The proper question to be asked as to a work of art is, '' What contagion of *feeling* does it communicate from the breast of the author to that of his audience?'' (Ib. 45.) The highest emotion which can be conveyed in this way is '' a sense of harmony or health of the Soul itself—the stirring within us of some divine and universal Being—to be capable of feeling which is indeed the most excellent prerogative of Man : a sense which we endeavor to express by the word Beauty, and the conveyance of which is the highest message of Art." (Ib. 78–9.) Carpenter never wanders far from this great thought; religion as well as art will eventually turn upon it.

The Religion of the future must come from the bosom itself of the modern peoples ; it must be the recognition by Humanity as a whole of that Common Life which has really underlain all the various religions of the past ; it must be the certainty of the organic unity of mankind, of the brotherhood of all sentient creatures, freeing itself from all local doctrine and prejudice, and expressing itself in any and every available form. The seal and sanction of the Art of the future will be its dedication to the service of this religion. (Ib. 135–6.)

The function of art "consists in actually drawing human beings together. . . To make mankind realize their unity, to make them *feel* it, that will be the inspiration and the province of art." (Ib 137.)

At the root of Beauty and the art sense Carpenter finds the sexual instincts, and in Love's Coming of Age he explains his views of these important matters from his new standpoint.

Sex is the allegory of Love in the physical world. It is from this fact that it derives its immense power. The

L. of C.

aim of Love is non-differentiation—absolute union of
being ; but absolute union can only be found at the center of existence.   Therefore whoever has truly found
another has found not only that other and with that other
himself, but has found also a third—who dwells at the
center and holds the plastic material of the universe in
the palm of his hand, and is a creator of sensible forms.
(Love's Coming of Age 20.)

In short, "the prime object of Sex is *union*," (Ib.
21), physical, mental, spiritual.   It is in subordination
to this conception that men should marry and give in
marriage, and it is easy for a writer who takes this high
ground to expose the shams involved in our present conventions, and it is natural that he should express the
hope for a more fluid, less rigid, state of society in the
future.   I should not recommend Carpenter (nor any
one else) as an infallible guide in this matter (nor in any
other), but his treatment of it is full of originality and
suggestion.

Carpenter's idea of sex as the basis of universal unity
naturally involves the question of the relationship to
each other of members of the same sex, as well as of
those of opposite sexes.   In his group of poems corre-
sponding to the Calamus of Whitman he celebrates com-
radeship in terms worthy of the ancient Greeks.   Such
sentiments are not often spoken of publicly in these days,
but it is irrational to condemn them offhand as inverted

and abnormal. All variations from the commonplace are abnormal, the good as well as the bad. Genius and philanthropy are abnormal, and the race would come to a standstill if it did not have such abnormal variations among which to choose its pathway. If, as Carpenter supposes—and with a good deal of plausibility—all affection has its basis in the sexual instincts, there is a degree of inversion in the love of father for son, of son for father, and of sisters for each other. Carpenter sees the drawbacks in our present system of intersexual relations, with its large proportion of unhappy marriages and the hypocrisy and suffering they entail—the binding together for life of illassorted pairs upon the false assumption that God has joined them, and the sickening cant which proscribes all attempts to look the situation in the face and find some remedy for it. He has manfully grappled with the problem and he deserves our thanks for his courage and frankness, but I do not believe that much is to be expected from close friendships of a romantic nature between persons of the same sex. Such friendships, as we often see them between young girls, involve all the jealousies and selfishness of normal courtship and have none of the physiological and domestic sanctions.

I confess that I feel no call to undertake the settlement of these troublesome questions of sex. In some future incarnation I may have them forced upon me, but for the present I see no solution and do not know in which direction to search for one.   Where divorce and promiscuity have become common, we see less contentment and more disorder.   Celibacy is sometimes proposed as the highest ideal, and we are told that to conceive of Christ, the perfect man, in the marriage relation, is to derogate from his dignity.   At first blush this seems true, and yet Christendom has refused to accept this celibate ideal and has provided the master with the church itself as a bride.   In doing so it has been in harmony with the universal rule of religious history, for the religious feelings, with their full flower of love to God and neighbor, seem everywhere grounded in sex. This, too, implies inversion, or rather development, in our primary instincts, and their extension from a single individual to all mankind.   It is possible that through its pioneers the race may advance from ordinary "falling in love" to a kindred passion for all life, and Carpenter's group of poems to which I have referred has a marked tendency in this direction, for he makes them culminate in a general, all-embracing love :

Oh, I am greedy of love—all, all are beautiful to me !
You are my deliverers every one—from death, from sin,
   from evil.
I float, I dissolve in you !—(Towards Democracy 286.)

And again :

So still to all—
To those lingering in prison,
To the aged and forsaken, stranded like wrecks on the
    bleak shores of life,
To the heartbroken and weary—to the stunned with
    despair, . . .
To you we give our love.   (Ib., 290.)

That Carpenter recognizes fully the beauty of the mono-
gamic ideal is shown by his poem The Golden Wedding.
(Ib. 306.)

We have now completed our review of the lifework of
this interesting man.   If there is a more significant figure in the England of today, I do not know it.   The
power of his character as revealed in his writings lies in
the fact that it is the fruit of a rich experience.   He
does not give us booklearning or fancy or speculation or
hypothesis, but like a traveler returning from a far
country he tells what he has seen and investigated.   If
he prefers the hard-working classes, it is because he
knows them intimately and finds them more truly men.
It is no imaginary theory à la Rousseau.

The fashionable, the intellectual and the commercial
classes are each narrowed down in their different ways
and along their own lines ; that greater class which lives
in more direct contact with Nature and the actual facts
of life seems to me (notwithstanding the specially trying
circumstances of its life at the present day) to be by far

the most *human ;* and I shall always be glad that I have come to know it, as I have done, and to learn some of the best lessons of my life from it. (England's Ideal 53–4.)

Thus enjoying the sense of universal unity in the bosom of the "lower" classes, Carpenter is passing his life, now and again acquainting such part of the world as may heed him with his discoveries and experiences. He finds particular pleasure in music, and a piano is among his few material treasures. He has edited Chants of Labor, and is the author and composer of the words and music of the fine socialist national anthem (if this be not a contradiction in terms) England Arise ! His de-votion to Beethoven, the democratic prince of musicmen, and his deep understanding of him, are shown in the la-ter essays of Angels' Wings. He is also, I am told, a personal friend of the first of living composers, the Nor-wegian Grieg, who is said to be of a radical turn of mind and more or less in sympathy with his English admirer. Carpenter has lately taken up with enthusiasm the cause of his dumb fellow creatures. Nor does he forget the oppressed peoples of the earth. His book of travels in India, From Adam's Peak to Elephanta, presents the unwonted spectacle of an Englishman actually regarding his Hindoo fellow subjects as friends and equals. It is characteristic of him that he finds more to commend in the Salvation Army in India than in any other British institution there established. The manual labor with which he diversifies his agricultural work—the manufacture of sandals—has as its object the freeing of the human foot from the stiff, impermeable leather boxes in which it is at present deformed and befouled. The boot is a symbol of the husks of which mankind must rid itself before it can attain to the human form divine and blossom into the long-awaited unity. When that day comes—when at last men's feet are shod with the winged sandals of Hermes which free and do not confine them—then we may be sure that the name of Edward Carpenter will be cherished as that of one of the guides and benefactors of the race, a true messenger of the gods and a healer of mankind.

Works of Edward Carpenter

Civilization.   Its Cause and Cure $1.06

"No passing piece of polemics, but a permanent possession."—
Scottish Review.

England's Ideal $1.05

"The literary power is unmistakable, their freshness of style,
their humor, and their enthusiasm."—*Pall Mall Gazette.*

Towards Democracy $2.12

"A remarkable work."—*Academy.*

EDWARD CARPENTER:
POET AND PROPHET

ERNEST CROSBY

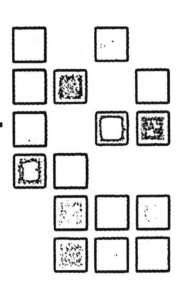

CPSIA information can be obtained
at www.ICGtesting.com
Printed in the USA
LVHW082337281220
675298LV00008B/105